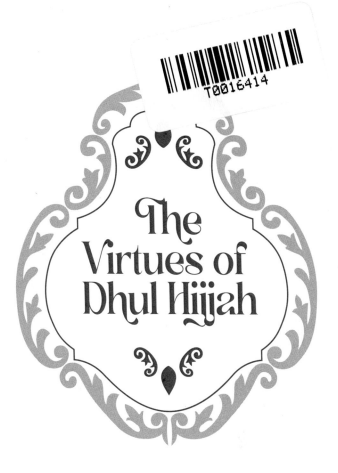

The Virtues of Dhul Hijjah

Omar Suleiman

KUBE
PUBLISHING

In association with

YAQEEN
INSTITUTE FOR ISLAMIC RESEARCH

The virtues of Dhul Hijjah

First published in England by
Kube Publishing Ltd
Markfield Conference Centre
Ratby Lane, Markfield
Leicestershire, LE67 9SY
United Kingdom

Tel: +44 (0) 1530 249230
Website: www.kubepublishing.com
Email: info@kubepublishing.com

Copyright © Omar Suleiman 2024
All Rights Reserved. 1st impression, 2024.

The right of Omar Suleiman to be identified as the author of
this work has been asserted by him in accordance with the Copyright, Design and Patent Act 1988.

Cataloguing-in-Publication Data is available from the British
Library.

ISBN 978-1-84774-225-4 Paperback
eISBN 978-1-84774-226-1 Ebook

Cover design and typesetting: Afreen Fazil (Jaryah Studios)
Printed in: Turkey, by Elma Basim

Proofreading and Editing by: Wordsmiths (www.wordsmiths.org.uk)

Contents

Preface

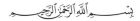

In the name of Allah,
the Most Gracious, the Most Merciful.

All praise is due to Allah ﷻ, and may His peace and blessings be upon the final Messenger Muhammad ﷺ, and all those who follow his way with righteousness until the end of time. Dhul Hijjah is one of the four Holy Months; it is a time of worship, sacrifice, and reflection. In this sacred month are the ten most blessed days of the year, and one of the two Eids.

Every year, millions of pilgrims gather to worship Allah ﷻ in Mecca during these blessed days. They travel from every corner of the world, responding to the call of Prophet Ibrāhīm ﷺ in order to worship Allah ﷻ through the rites of Hajj. There, in the fields of Minā and Muzdalifah, and around the Mountain of ʿArafah, they engage in deep acts of worship, calling on their Lord, seeking forgiveness and answers to their prayers.

The blessings of Dhul Hijjah are not limited to those who are blessed with responding to the call for Hajj. Every Muslim, wherever they are in the world, can benefit from these blessed days. In this book, we will explore some of the profound virtues of Dhul Hijjah and the blessings associated with it. Together, we hope to revive the tradition of dedicating these beautiful days to worshipping Allah ﷻ and gaining His Favour.

Allah ﷻ has blessed us with a twelve-month lunar calendar beginning with Muḥarram and ending with Dhul Hijjah. That the calendar ends with Dhul Hijjah signifies that the new year inaugurates a state of sinlessness for many people entering the new year, as they are purified through their Hajj and worship. Just as every accepted Hajj leads to the pilgrim returning home as sinless as a newborn baby, likewise, the new year is a sign of new beginnings and a renewed hope for every believer.

Ibn 'Abbās ⬥ reported that the Prophet ﷺ said: 'No good deeds are better than what is done in these first ten days of Dhul Hijjah.' (*Bukhārī*)

Let us explore the virtues and blessings of these blessed days together.

We ask Allah ﷻ to accept our efforts and add them to our scales on the Last Day.

Your Brother,

Omar Suleiman

The Sacred Months

The Prophet ﷺ declared: 'The year is composed of twelve months, of which four are sacred: the three consecutive months of Dhul Qaʿdah, Dhul Hijjah, and Muḥarram; and Rajab, which comes between Jumādā [al-Thāniyah] and Shaʿbān.' (*Bukhārī*)

With a very specific type of sanctity in mind, we often default to Ramadan when thinking of the sacred months in our Islamic calendar. As the holiest and most virtuous month of the year, it is understandable why Ramadan immediately comes to mind. However, the four sacred months mentioned by the Prophet ﷺ – Dhul Qaʿdah, Dhul Hijjah, Muḥarram, and Rajab – also contain their own invaluable virtues, practices, and lessons that are important for us to take seriously and be aware of.

Without knowing these sacred months by name, failing to learn where they are positioned in the Islamic calendar and neglecting to understand their characteristics, we can often overlook their unique merits. For example, when thinking of the month in which fasting is seen as the most virtuous act outside of Ramadan, most people would immediately think of Shaʿbān or Shawwāl and the six days one is encouraged to fast therein. In fact, the Prophet ﷺ stated that the most beneficial month of fasting – or the month in which fasting is most beloved to Allah ﷻ – after Ramadan is Muḥarram, which is known as the month of Allah ﷻ. This should reveal the importance of truly coming to know these months and of understanding what they represent.

Historical context

The four sacred months were the months in which fighting and all forms of battle were prohibited, even by the pre-Islamic Arabs. The sacred months all possess special meanings, and their names typically relate to historic seasons of warfare, often referring to practices or events that would take place. Dhul Qaʿdah means 'the month to sit', indicating that one essentially sits back and does not engage in fighting or warfare. Dhul Hijjah is the month in which Hajj takes place; even in the pre-Islamic days of ignorance there used to be a yearly pilgrimage. Muḥarram means 'forbidden', and marks the beginning of the year with abstinence from warfare. Rajab, which is the only month that does not come in succession with the other three sacred months, means 'to remove and refrain' – so you would remove your weapons and refrain from fighting in the middle of the year.

The successional separation of Rajab is beautifully described by Imam al-Shāfiʿī ☙, who likened it to the position of ʿUmar ibn ʿAbd al-ʿAzīz ☙ in relation to the rest of the Khulafāʾ al-Rāshidūn (the Rightly-Guided Caliphs). ʿUmar ibn ʿAbd al-ʿAzīz ☙, although he did not live immediately after ʿAlī ☙ or assume leadership immediately after him, is still included amongst the Khulafāʾ

al-Rāshidūn despite his chronological separation from them.

Before the advent of Islam, the pagan Arabs would shift the order of the sacred months around, repositioning them so that they could structure the year around their fighting. If they needed to change a month so that they could engage in battle or afford themselves flexibility at certain times of the year, they would not hesitate to do so. Because of this, Allah ﷻ fixed the order of all months and informed us of the special rules and virtues pertaining to each of them.

Upon reflection, it is apparent that there is much benefit and wisdom in the order that Allah ﷻ chose for these months. Ramadan is succeeded by the six days of fasting in Shawwāl. Immediately after this comes Dhul Qaʿdah – a sacred month allowing you to prepare yourself for Hajj, which occurs in the next consecutive month of Dhul Hijjah. Dhul Hijjah is marked by an array of virtues In its first ten days, which include the Day of ʿArafah, Eid, and many more opportunities for righteousness, and is succeeded by Muḥarram – the best month to fast outside of Ramadan. The order of months gives the believer the opportunity to maintain his spiritual high throughout the year, capitalising on each unique virtue of the sacred months in quick succession. You finish the Islamic year strong in Ramadan, Shawwāl, Dhul Qaʿdah, and Dhul Hijjah, after which you are able to start the Islamic year strong with Muḥarram and sustain this spirit of righteousness throughout Rajab.

Multiplied deeds

Aside from the sanctity of life represented by the cessation of warfare, there are other practical considerations more relevant to the lives of contemporary believers that the sacred months give rise to. During these months, good deeds are more beneficial and blessed, so Allah ﷻ multiplies the rewards of any good deeds performed within them. Parallel to this, sins are amplified or considered worse in these months, and this has been passed down in a saying of al-Ḥāfiẓ Ibn Rajab ﷺ, who said:

احْذُرُوا المَعَاصِي فَإِنَّهَا تَحْرِمُ الْمَغْفِرَةَ فِيْ مَوَاسِمِ الرَّحْمَةِ

'Be careful of the acts of disobedience because verily they forbid forgiveness in the seasons of mercy.'

So, just as committing a sin in prayer is worse than committing a sin outside of prayer, committing a sin within the sacred months is worse than doing so at any other time of the year. Allah gives us seasons of mercy and forgiveness, and it is incumbent upon us to capitalise on these opportunities, making sure that we do not do anything that will cause us to be deprived of the blessings and rewards of these holy months.

Dhul Hijjah stands as the most sacred of all the sacred months. The Prophet ﷺ said in a Hadith narrated by Abū Bakr ﷺ: 'No doubt, your blood, your property, and your honour are sacred to one another like the sanctity of this day of yours, in this month of yours, in this place of yours [Mecca]'. The Prophet ﷺ informed us that the most sacred day is the Day of ʿArafah, that the most sacred month is Dhul Hijjah, and the most sacred place is al-Masjid al-Ḥarām – the most sanctified place.

In order to reap the blessings and rewards of these sacred months, and to avoid what is forbidden and disliked within them, it is vital that we familiarise ourselves with the Islamic calendar. With this intention, we ask Allah ﷻ to allow us to achieve the benefits, mercy, and forgiveness bestowed upon the righteous within these months, and to allow us to abstain from sin throughout the entire year. *Āmīn.*

2

The Most Virtuous Days

Ibn 'Abbās ⬚ reported that the Prophet ⬚ said: 'No good deeds are better than what is done in these first ten days of Dhul Hijjah.' Some Companions of the Prophet ⬚ then said: 'Not even jihad in the way of Allah?' The Prophet ⬚ said: 'Not even jihad in the way of Allah, except for a man who goes out with his life and wealth at risk and he returns with nothing.' (*Bukhārī*)

The Prophet ⬚ stated that there is no deed better in the sight of Allah ⬚ or more greatly rewarded by Him than a good deed that is done in the first 10 days of Dhul Hijjah. The only exception is for one who performs jihad in the path of Allah ⬚, sacrificing his life and wealth for that cause. The term jihad refers to striving or a noble struggle, and thus here the Prophet ﷺ is referring to a person who goes out and loses everything, meaning that they sacrifice their lives and their wealth in pursuit of this noble cause.

Some scholars have said that this Hadith refers to Muṣ'ab ibn 'Umayr ﷺ becoming Muslim and, as a result, being persecuted in Mecca. Muṣ'ab ibn 'Umayr ﷺ was the richest and wealthiest man in Mecca – a trendsetter of sorts. He was a young man that everyone looked up to; he had the most expensive smelling perfumes and the most beautiful of clothes, but was persecuted and driven out of Mecca owing to his submission to Islam. Muṣ'ab ﷺ migrated to Medina with the Prophet ﷺ and was the first to introduce Islam to the people of Medina. He was subsequently killed in the Battle of Uḥud, a day on which the defeated Muslims could not even find enough cloth to cover his entire body. This man literally sacrificed everything and is said to be the mani-festation of the one 'who goes out with his life and wealth at risk and he returns with nothing'.

In another Hadith, the Prophet ﷺ was asked about what the best form of struggle or jihad in the path of Allah ﷻ is and described a person who goes out and in the process of battle loses absolutely everything.

So, what does this mean for us when we are contemplating the first ten days of Dhul Hijjah? The Prophet ﷺ essentially informed us that good deeds performed in these ten days are not just better than jihad in the path of Allah ﷻ but are one of the best forms of jihad in the path of Allah ﷻ. The scholars concluded from this narration that the Prophet ﷺ telling us that good deeds performed in the first ten days of Dhul Hijjah surpass good deeds performed in any other ten days of the year – an understanding similar to the superiority of *dhikr* (the remembrance of Allah ﷻ) over jihad in the path of Allah ﷻ apparent in certain contexts and narrations that have reached us from the Prophet ﷺ.

In another Hadith, the Prophet ﷺ was asked what the best deeds are. He mentioned: 'To have faith in Allah'. Then he was asked: 'Then what?' He mentioned first: 'Jihad in the path of Allah'. Thereafter he was asked: 'Then what?' He said: 'The Hajj'. (*Bukhārī* 1519; *Muslim* 83) Here, the Prophet ﷺ has informed us about the superiority of good deeds performed during the first ten days of Dhul Hijjah over any other days, such that any good deed that you do in these ten days would surpass even the best of righteous deeds performed in other circumstances.

Why are these days so virtuous?

Scholars mention a few reasons as to why these days are considered so special. Firstly, in Sūrah al-Māʾidah, Allah ﷻ says:

$$ لْيَوْمَ أَكْمَلْتُ لَكُمْ دِينَكُمْ وَأَتْمَمْتُ عَلَيْكُمْ نِعْمَتِي وَرَضِيتُ لَكُمُ الْإِسْلَمَ دِينًا $$

'This day I have perfected for you your religion, completed My favour upon you, and have chosen for you Islam as your religion.' (al-Māʾidah, 3)

Based on this, scholars have derived the conclusion that the fact that Allah ﷻ completed and perfected the religion for us within these 10 days is, in and of itself, an indication of its virtue.

Ibn Ḥajar ؓ also said that all good deeds are combined in these 10 days in a way unalike any other time. Most significantly, we can see the manifestation of the five pillars of Islam during this period. We have the testimony of the Oneness of Allah ﷻ and following the Messenger ﷺ; prayers, which are given extra attention by countless Muslims; Hajj, which cannot be done at any other time of the year; charity, which is constantly being performed during these 10 days – most uniquely in the form of sacrificing a goat, sheep, cow or camel; and fasting, a Sunnah encouraged by our Prophet ﷺ, who would fast the first nine days and who told us that fasting the Day of ʿArafah expiates the sins of two years: the past year and the coming one (*Muslim*).

This combination of all the pillars of Islam manifesting in the first ten days of Dhul Hijjah is unique and cannot be found during any other ten days of the year.

Increase your Worship

Imam Ḥasan al-Baṣrī ﷺ was asked: 'What are the best things that we can do in these ten days?' He responded: 'Firstly, do not lose your obligations. Do not lose your obligations because these ten days celebrate the obligations – the pillars of Islam. So do not lose your obligations. Thereafter, the second thing to do is increase your good deeds, because during these ten days, the good deeds that are done are unlike good deeds done at any other time.'

When we look at the Companions of the Messenger ﷺ and the pious predecessors, we really start to see how seriously they took these ten days, pushing themselves in ways that we would not typically push ourselves today. In Ramadan, the feeling of togetherness in worship is ubiquitous – everyone is fasting, praying, and pushing themselves to perform all types of good deeds together. Nevertheless, in the first ten days of Dhul Hijjah, you do not typically see people exerting themselves the way that they would in Ramadan because there is no community exertion.

However, we find a very different approach amongst the stories of the Companions. Saʿīd ibn Jubayr ﷺ related that Ibn ʿAbbās ﷺ and his father, who narrated this Hadith, used to disappear in the first 10 days of Dhul Hijjah. They were so busy performing good deeds in these ten days that no one could reach them during this period (*Fatḥ al-Bārī*).

We typically examine individuals who narrated Hadith to discern how those narrators implemented the content of the Hadith they narrate, and when we look at the significance of Ibn ʿAbbās ﷺ in relation to narrations regarding Dhul Hijjah, what we find is truly beautiful. Not only do we find that he was the foremost narrator of the Prophet's ﷺ message about the virtues of these ten days, but also that he was nearly impossible to reach in these ten days because of how much he would busy himself with worship.

We ask Allah ﷻ to allow us to fulfil our obligations and avoid all forms of disobedience; we ask Him to increase our good deeds in these ten days in a manner that would not occur at any other time of the year, whilst also ensuring that we do not neglect these good deeds during other times of the year. *Āmīn*.

This day I have
perfected for you
your religion
and completed My
favour upon you
and have chosen
for you Islam as
your religion

3

The Days
Allah Swears By

وَٱلْفَجْرِ ۞ وَلَيَالٍ عَشْرٍ ۞ وَٱلشَّفْعِ وَٱلْوَتْرِ ۞
وَٱلَّيْلِ إِذَا يَسْرِ ۞

By the dawn, by ten nights, by the even and the odd,
by the passing night. (89: 1-4)

We often hear that Allah ﷻ swears by ten
nights, and as such, it's important that
we explore the virtues and benefits of this oath,
considering the significance of why Allah ﷻ
swears by these nights. According to the majority
of scholars, and in the opinion of Imam al-Ṭabarī
ﷺ the consensus of scholars, the ten nights that
Allah ﷻ swears by in Sūrah al-Fajr are the first
ten nights of Dhul Hijjah. It merits mention that

some scholars hold a minority opinion that this Qur'anic expression refers to the last ten nights of Ramadan, with some further mentioning the absence of a definite article in 'by ten nights' to be evidence that the expression could refer to two sets of ten nights – the last ten of Ramadan and the first ten of Dhul Hijjah. Nevertheless, according to the vast majority of scholars, this oath is said to refer to the ten days that mark the beginning of Dhul Hijjah – another sign of the virtue of this time.

You might wonder about the seemingly inter-changeable use of the words 'night' and 'day' employed when referring to these periods of time. Scholars of the Arabic language and the Qur'an will point to the fact that the words 'night' and 'day' in Arabic are often interchangeable in terms of their use, with rhetorical factors such as eloquence or flow determining the appro-priateness of either one. For example, this is apparent in the story of the Prophet Zakariyyā ⒔ in the Qur'an. Allah ⒔ speaks about the Prophet Zakariyyā ⒔ and the duration of his oath of silence. In one place, Allah ﷻ refers to this period of time as 'three nights' (*Maryam* 19:10) and as 'three days' in another place (*Āl ʿImrān* 3:41). This interchangeability between the terms night and day is a linguistic characteristic that exists in the Qur'an and is often witnessed in Arabic literature. Therefore, although Allah ﷻ swears by ten nights, this expression likewise refers to the first ten days of Dhul Hijjah. As such, we know decisively that the most virtuous nights of the year are the last ten nights of Ramadan and the most virtuous days of the year are the first ten days of Dhul Hijjah.

Other scholars have also opined that when Allah ﷻ swears by the dawn, He is in fact swearing by the dawn of the Day of Eid, which is right after the Day of ʿArafah and the Day of Sacrifice. Accordingly, Allah ﷻ is also swearing by a very particular dawn in the month of Dhul Hijjah.

The Best of Times

In the aforementioned verses, Allah ﷻ swears by the best part of the day (the dawn) before swearing by the best days of the year (the ten nights), after which He swears by the best days of those days (the even and the odd) and, finally, by the best part of the night (the passing night).

Firstly, Allah ﷻ swears by the dawn (*fajr*), the best and most blessed part of the day. The Prophet ﷺ said: 'Allah has placed blessing in the early morning hours'. There are things that can be done between dawn and sunrise that cannot be done throughout the day. This is a time during which you will find your greatest energy and deeds amplified – an opportunity to start the day off right! We learn that even sitting in the mosque and remembering Allah ﷻ between dawn and sunrise earns a reward equivalent to Hajj, as mentioned by the Prophet ﷺ (*Tirmidhī*, 586). This time is the most blessed part of the day, though it represents an opportunity missed by many people.

Allah ﷻ then swears by the most blessed days of the year – the first ten days of Dhul Hijjah – before swearing by the most blessed days of those ten days. According to narrations, the Qur'anic expression 'the even and the odd' either refers to the day of Eid or the Day of Sacrifice (Yawm al-Naḥr) as the even (10th of Dhul Hijjah), and the Day of ʿArafah which is the most blessed day on the 9th day of Dhul Hijjah as the odd.

Allah ﷻ then swears specifically by the night as it starts to leave you (the passing night), meaning the last part of the night. This time is the time of *qiyām al-layl*, the most blessed time to pray, and the time of *suḥūr,* the best time to eat if one intends to fast. It may be said that in these last parts of the night, we feed ourselves spiritually and physically for the sake of Allah ﷻ.

Furthermore, it merits mention that some scholars of exegesis also interpreted the third verse of Sūrah al-Burūj to be a reference to a day within the blessed days of Dhul Hijjah.

Allah ﷺ says:

وَشَاهِدٍ وَمَشهودٍ

'And [by] the witness and what is witnessed.'
(al-Burūj, 3)

'The witness' here refers to the days of ʿArafah and Jumuʿah, as the Day of ʿArafah and the Day of Jumuʿah share many similar traits: just as the Day of ʿArafah is the best day of the year, the Day of Jumuʿah is the best day of the week; just as the period between ʿAsr and Maghrib is a time during which we should increase in our supplications on the Day of ʿArafah, it is also a period – according to an authentic narration – on the Day of Jumuʿah during which we should increase our supplications to Allah ﷺ.

Abū Hurayrah ﷺ reported: 'The Messenger of Allah ﷺ mentioned the day of Friday and he said, "In it is an hour in which no Muslim stands to pray and ask Allah for something but that he will be given it," and he indicated with his hand that the time is very short.' (*Bukhārī*, 935; *Muslim*, 852).

In mentioning and swearing in this fashion, Allah ﷻ has honoured these times of the day, times of the year, and times of the night, and there are many lessons we can take from this. If we are truly among the elect people who seek the blessings of Allah ﷻ, then we should always seek to get ahead by making use of the blessed seasons Allah ﷻ has provided for us. Evidently, our Lord does not lack in mercy or justice – instead, it is due to our own negligence of these blessed times that we may fall behind. Unfortunately, most people do not do anything spectacular in terms of their level of remembrance nor in terms of their good deeds. As such, we need to remind ourselves of the ample opportunities to please Allah ﷻ afforded to us.

Thus, if you really want to shine in the sight of Allah ﷻ, then capitalise on His blessed seasons. Wake up a little bit before Fajr when most people are still sleeping and invoke Allah ﷻ at a time when Allah ﷻ truly favours His chosen servants.

After Fajr, when most people go back to sleep, shine – get a head start on your good deeds; get a head start on your productivity! Take advantage of these ten days, which are better than the entire year.

This is your time to shine. Do not lose the opportunity.

4

The Prophetic Connections

Many of us are not in the habit of connecting our good deeds, those performed following the way of the Prophet Muhammad ﷺ, with the Prophets who came before him. We are unaware of the significant spiritual overlap that exists between our prophetic traditions. However, by understanding these connections we will be able to foster a deeper spiritual connection with all of the Prophets, thereby gaining a better understanding of the manner in which Allah ﷻ allowed particular times and deeds to coincide with one another. In line with the following Hadith, one such connection that often surprises people is the fact that all the holy books were revealed within the month of Ramadan, not just the Qur'an:

Allah's Messenger ﷺ said: 'The Ṣuḥuf (Scrolls) of Ibrāhīm ﷺ were revealed during the first night of Ramadan. The Tawrāh (Torah) was revealed during the sixth night of Ramadan. The Injīl (Gospel) was revealed during the thirteenth night of Ramadan. The Zabūr (Psalms of David) were revealed on the eighteenth of Ramadan. And Allah revealed the Qur'an on the twenty-fourth night of Ramadan.' (Aḥmad)

The holy books sent to Ibrāhīm, Mūsā, ʿĪsā, Dāwūd, and the Prophet Muhammad ﷺ were all revealed during the month of Ramadan. Allah ﷻ chose that blessed month to coincide with the time during which all holy books would be revealed, not just the Qur'an. From this, we can see there is a deep spiritual connection that spans across our prophetic history.

Connecting Prophets to Dhul Hijjah

Similarly, when we think of Hajj, we think of Prophet Ibrāhīm ﷺ and his raising of the foundations of the Ka'bah, but seldom do we consider that the foundations he raised were those built for Adam and Ḥawwā ﷺ by the Angels in the location where they first resided on earth. This sense of continuity is reinforced in narrations in which the Prophet Muhammad ﷺ mentions Prophets who visited the sacred spaces of Mecca or made Hajj or 'Umrah at some point in their lives – specifically, the Prophet ﷺ mentioned the Prophets Hūd and Mūsā ﷺ having done so. With this under consideration, our appreciation and perspective of the immense sanctity of the Hajj ought to heighten as we imagine Prophet Mūsā ﷺ making *ṭawāf* around the Ka'bah, the very temple that was established by his grandfather and the grandfather of the Prophet Muhammad ﷺ, Ibrāhīm ﷺ. Our spiritual connection with our prophetic lineage further intensifies when we consider that Prophet Ibrāhīm ﷺ raised the sacred house with his son Ismāʿīl ﷺ, and that other Prophets honoured this ancient sanctuary by visiting and circumambulating it.

As was mentioned, the Prophet Muhammad ﷺ informed us of the Prophet Mūsā's ﷺ visit to Mecca. In addition to this, a further narration informs us that Prophet Mūsā ﷺ asked Allah ﷻ what the best form of remembrance was on the Day of ʿArafah – a day already recognised for its importance. He was told to say *'lā ilāha illā Allāh'* (there is no god but Allah alone) – the testimony of faith that bears witness to the Oneness of Allah ﷻ. This is because, when we were extracted from the back of Prophet Adam ﷺ on that day, we all testified to the Oneness of Allah ﷻ. As such, the best form of remembrance on the Day of ʿArafah is testifying to the Oneness of Allah ﷻ in any way.

The Prophet ﷺ said: 'The best supplication is that which is made on the Day of ʿArafah. The best of it is what was said by myself and the Prophets before me. "There is no god but Allah alone, without any partners, unto Him belong all dominion and praise, and He has power over all things'" (*Tirmidhī*).

We are told to bear witness to the Oneness of Allah ﷻ just as we bore witness on the day when we were originally brought into being. We must testify that He has no partner, that He is alone in His Dominion, that He is most worthy of praise, and that He has power over all things. Significantly, this is considered the best form of supplication or remembrance that the Prophet ﷺ taught us, as it was prefaced by a declaration that he ﷺ and the Prophets before him did not say anything better than this. On the Day of 'Arafah, in order to remember the day we were extracted from the back of the Prophet Adam ﷺ, all of the Prophets regularly recited these testimonies of faith.

The ten days of Prophet Musa ﷺ

There is another interesting connection between Prophet Mūsā ﷺ and Dhul Hijjah apparent in the Qur'an. According to the majority of scholars,

Eid al-Adha was the very day that Allah ﷻ spoke directly to Mūsā ﷺ. We see in Sūrah al-A'rāf that Allah mentions the forty days of fasting performed by Mūsā ﷺ:

$$وَوَاعَدْنَا مُوسٰى ثَلٰثِيْنَ لَيْلَةً وَّ اَتْمَمْنٰهَا بِعَشْرٍ فَتَمَّ مِيْقَاتُ رَبِّهٖۤ اَرْبَعِيْنَ لَيْلَةً$$

'And We made an appointment with Moses for thirty nights and perfected them by [the addition of] ten; so the term of his Lord was completed as forty nights.' (al-A'rāf, 142)

The biblical narrative presented in *Exodus* 34:28 states: 'Moses was there with the Lord 40 days and 40 nights without eating bread or drinking water, and he wrote the tablets in the words of the Covenant.' In accordance with the Qur'an, Musa initially had thirty days of fasting and then Allah ﷻ gave him an additional ten days, during which he completed the forty nights with Allah ﷻ. In the next verse, Allah ﷻ then describes the conversation that took place:

وَلَمَّا جَاءَ مُوسَىٰ لِمِيقَٰتِنَا وَكَلَّمَهُ رَبُّهُ

'And when Moses arrived at Our appointed time and his Lord spoke to him, he said, "My Lord, show me [Yourself] that I may look at You."' (al-Aʿrāf, 143)

Scholars concluded that the initial thirty days of Mūsā's ﷺ fasting were the days of Dhul Qāʿdah, and accordingly, the subsequent ten days coincided with the first ten days of Dhul Hijjah. The profound conversation between Creator and creation and the awesome theophany directed towards the mountain marked the end of the ten days of Dhul Hijjah that Prophet Mūsā ﷺ spent fasting.

As Muslims, our connection to these prophetic experiences must be strong. Not so long ago, we fasted thirty days of Ramadan and then, thanks to the most virtuous days of the year, Allah ﷻ bestowed upon us another ten days in Dhul Hijjah to draw near unto Him and take full advantage of the blessings on offer. Considering the post-Ramadan dip in our motivation, actions, or goals frequently experienced, these ten days are the perfect opportunity to revitalise our connection with our Creator.

As we perform good deeds in these ten days, remembering the Prophets that came before us and their momentous journeys to the Kaʿbah which culminated in their devotions on the Day of ʿArafah will heighten our spiritual connection to both Allah ﷻ and His Messengers ﷺ. In particular, remembering Prophet Mūsā ﷺ, his fasting, and how Allah ﷻ honoured him by speaking to him directly on the Day of Eid al-Adha will serve to strengthen our bonds to the prophetic legacy.

May Allah ﷻ allow us to meet Him on the Day of Judgement while He is pleased with us. May He allow us to see Him on the Day of Judgement while He is pleased with us, and may He allow us to be joined with all of the Prophets in the highest level of Jannah al-Firdaws, staring and gazing upon Him. *Āmīn.*

5

Fasting the First 9 Days

The Prophet ﷺ was in the habit of fasting numerous days throughout the year. Hunaydah ibn Khālid narrated from his wife, on the authority of one of the Mothers of the Believers ﷺ that: 'The Messenger of Allah ﷺ used to fast the first nine days of Dhul Hijjah, 'Āshūrā', and three days of every lunar month: the first Monday of the month and two Thursdays' (*Nasā'ī*, 2417).

Although typically speaking, we tend to fast on the Day of 'Arafah, oftentimes failing to take into account the first eight days of Dhul Hijjah, this Hadith demonstrates that the Prophet ﷺ would in fact fast all nine days. He also used to fast on the Day of ʿĀshūrā', which occurs in Muḥarram – the very next month – in commemoration of the victory of Mūsā ﷺ over Pharaoh. This Hadith also states that the Prophet ﷺ would habitually fast three further days of each lunar month: the 13th, 14th and 15th of each month, which are called *ayyām al-bīḍ* (the white days) due to the fullness of the moon at this time (*Abū Dāwūd*, 2449). In this narration, it is also apparent that the Prophet ﷺ would fast the first Monday of the month and two Thursdays. The Prophet ﷺ used to fast on Mondays and Thursdays because deeds are presented to Allah ﷺ on these days, and as such he hoped that his deeds would be presented to Allah ﷺ whilst in a state of fasting. He ﷺ also designated Monday as a day of fasting because he was born on this day and would fast in submission to Allah ﷺ as an expression of his gratitude for this. (*Tirmidhī*, 747)

Considering this narration, it is apparent that the Prophet ﷺ was in the habit of fasting numerous days throughout the year. In contradiction to the aforementioned narrations, however, there is a report from 'Ā'ishah 🌸 indicating that the Prophet 🌸 did *not* fast all of the first nine days of Dhul Hijjah. Scholars reconcile these seemingly contradictory Hadiths by concluding that the Prophet 🌸 did not fast every single day of the nine, but certainly fasted a lot of them. It was an established habit of the Messenger 🌸 to fast during the first nine days of Dhul Hijjah, not limiting his fasting to the 9th of Dhul Hijjah – the Day of 'Arafah – alone.

Combining intentions, maximising reward

Good deeds are especially beloved to Allah 🌸 in these ten days, and as such, we should perform as many of them as possible, especially when it comes to fasting. 'Umar ibn al-Khaṭṭāb 🌸 narrated: 'I heard Allah's Messenger 🌸 saying, "The reward of deeds depends upon their intentions, and every person will get a reward according to what he has intended. So, as for whoever has emigrated for worldly benefits or for a woman to marry, his emigration was for what he emigrated for."'

One of the blessings given to us by Allah ﷻ is that we find rewards in combining intentions for multiple voluntary good deeds. Firstly, within a voluntary good deed, we could have multiple intentions that make the reward of that deed doubly blessed. For example, the Prophet ﷺ mentioned two separate intentions for fasting on Mondays: firstly, because deeds are presented to Allah ﷻ on that day and secondly, because the Prophet ﷺ was born on that day. Here, we find two noble intentions combined within the same voluntary good deed.

Furthermore, one is able to combine intentions for voluntary good deeds that would otherwise be separate. For example, when you walk into the mosque, you can combine the intention for *taḥi-yyah al-masjid* – the two units to be prayed upon entering the *masjid* – with, for example, the two *sunnah* units of Fajr. If you pray two units with this combined intention, you will be rewarded for both the *taḥiyyah al-masjid* and the *sunnah* units of Fajr, God willing.

Likewise, when it comes to fasting, we can combine our intentions to perform multiple good deeds. For example, if one or more of the first nine days of Dhul Hijjah is a Monday or a Thursday, we can fast such days with the intention of them being both one of the first ten days of Dhul Hijjah and a Monday or a Thursday. We fast one day and, by the grace of Allah 🕮, gain the blessings of two occasions! Combining intentions enables us to amplify our rewards in the sight of Allah 🕮.

Within the blessed days of Dhul Hijjah there are multiple intentions that can be combined to maximise reward. We have the opportunity to fast with the intention of following the Sunnah of the Prophet 🕮 and Mūsā 🕮, of reaping the virtues of the first ten days of Dhul Hijjah, of emulating the Sunnah of fasting on Monday and/or a Thursday, and in hope that Allah 🕮 will see our deeds and be pleased with us!

Accordingly, if you are looking for a few days to fast within these nine days but are unable to fast all of them or many of them, then this is the perfect opportunity to combine several good intentions and fast on a Monday and/or Thursday before the ultimate Day of 'Arafah, on which all those capable of fasting should be doing so, by the grace of Allah ﷻ.

We ask Allah ﷻ to accept all of our good deeds and our fasting in these 10 days. *Āmīn*.

The Preferred Forms of Remembrance

The Prophet ﷺ said: 'There are no days that are greater in the sight of Allah ﷻ, or in which good deeds are more beloved to Him, than these ten days, so recite a great deal of *tahlīl* (*lā ilāha illā Allāh* – there is no god except Allah), *takbīr* (*Allāhu akbar* – Allah is Most Great) and *taḥmīd* (*alḥamdulillāh* – all praise is due to Allah) during them.' (*Aḥmad*)

Here, the Prophet ﷺ specifically emphasises that we need to increase in our remembrance of Allah in these ten days, teaching us the phrases that we should typically recite. In another narration, the Prophet ﷺ also taught us that 'the best way to celebrate the remembrance of Allah ﷻ is to say:

"*lā ilāha illā Allāh* (there is no god except Allah)'"
(*Tirmidhī*). Evidently, there is immense significance in keeping our tongues moist by perpet-
ually chanting *lā ilāha illā Allāh* and in being in
constant remembrance of Allah ﷻ during this
sacred season.

As many scholars have pointed out, in this Hadith,
the Prophet ﷺ also indicates the importance of
quantity in his command to 'recite a great deal'.
Undeniably, the quality of those affirmations
matter, but the Prophet's ﷺ direct emphasis on
the number of times we should mention these
phrases of remembrance should be heeded,
particularly in these ten blessed days.

Practices of the pious predecessors

There are many practical strategies that we can
implement derived from narrations detailing how
our pious predecessors engaged in the remembrance of Allah ﷻ. For example, it is narrated in
Ṣaḥīḥ al-Bukhārī that, in the first 10 days of Dhul

Hijjah, ʿAbdullāh ibn ʿUmar, his father, and Abū
Hurayrah ﷺ used to go out in the market place
and constantly chant *takbir* as follows: *Allāhu
akbar, Allāhu akbar, lā ilāha illā Allāh, wa Allāhu
akbar, wa li Allāh al-ḥamd* (Allah is Most Great,
Allah is Most Great, there is no god except Allah,
Allah is Most Great, Allah is Most Great, all praise
to Allah). While these are the phrases that we
all generally hear only on the Day of Eid, it was
the practice of these Companions ﷺ to recite
this specific formulation of glory throughout the
marketplace during all ten days of Dhul Hijjah.
It has also been narrated that the people around
them would join in their devotions and recite the
takbīr as well.

The point to be stressed here is that we should
increase our engagement in the forms of *dhikr*
during these times, and just as our predecessors
would recite them loudly in the marketplace to
remind everyone else to do so, we should fill our
time with the audible remembrance of Allah
ﷺ. within our homes and around our families.
We should recite the *takbīr* at every opportunity,

whether we are going in and out of the mosque, before and after our prayers, or walking through the streets, thus re-emphasising this practice of making a repeated form of *dhikr* – one that we find in the Sunnah, yet one that is so often abandoned, particularly in these 10 days.

These words of remembrance also connect us in a special way with the Prophet Ibrāhīm ☙, the Prophet most honoured after the Prophet Muhammad ☙, within these 10 days. In a conversation between Prophet Ibrāhīm and Prophet Muhammad ☙ on the night of Isrā' and Miʿrāj, these words of remembrance were conveyed to the Chosen One ☙ in the form of advice from that great patriarch of Arabs and Israelites alike. Ibn Masʿūd ☙ reported that the Prophet ☙ said:

'I met Ibrāhīm on the Night of Ascension and he said to me: "O Muhammad, convey my greetings to your nation, and tell them that Paradise has pure soil and sweet water. It is a vast plain land and its seedlings are: *subḥān Allāh* (glory be to Allah), *al-ḥamd li Allāh* (praise be to Allah), and *lā ilāha illā Allāh* (there is no god but Allah), and *Allāhu akbar* (Allah is the Greatest)'" (*Tirmidhī*).

The seeds of these plants in Paradise are utterances of remembrance. So, these forms of *dhikr* that we regularly recite are seeds meant to be planted in the very soil of Jannah. In essence, the Prophet Ibrāhīm ﷺ sent his greetings of peace to us, and then reminded us to say these words frequently, because doing so will allow us to plant trees under which we will relax in Jannah.

If this is the magnitude of such words of remembrance throughout the year, then consider their weight during these ten holy days regarding which the Prophet ﷺ explicitly commanded us to be plentiful in our *dhikr,* and to make sure that we recite these specific forms of remembrance constantly throughout our days! We ask Allah ﷻ to accept our remembrance throughout these ten days and beyond them, and to allow us to keep our tongues moist with the remembrance of our Lord and keep our hearts saturated in them. *Āmīn*.

The Sacrifice

The most significant religious practice that is performed within the ten days of Dhul Hijjah is undoubtedly the sacrifice on Eid al-Adha commemorating the sacrifice of the Prophet Ibrāhīm ﷺ. In the pre-Islamic context, *uḍḥiyyah* (sacrifice) was performed for the idols that once surrounded the Ka'bah. This form of worship was deeply embedded into pre-Islamic practices, and so, in response, Allah ﷻ commands us to rectify our intentions in Sūrah al-A'rāf:

قُلْ إِنَّ صَلَاتِي وَنُسُكِي وَمَحْيَايَ وَمَمَاتِي لِلّٰهِ رَبِّ لْعَٰلَمِينَ

'Say: "Indeed, my prayer, my rites of sacrifice, my living and my dying are for Allah, Lord of the worlds."' (al-A'rāf, 162)

The fact that Allah ﷻ puts sacrifice in the same category as prayer bears testament to how deeply entrenched it was as an act of worship to the idols. Embedded in Judeo-Christian thought in the conception of the Prophet Ibrāhīm's ﷺ trial and ʿĪsā ﷺ as the lamb of Allah ﷻ, the notion of sacrifice for the sake of Allah ﷻ has a primordial meaning present in all Abrahamic faith communities. For us as Muslims, first and foremost, we conceive of sacrifice as a means of drawing close to Allah ﷻ. The words *qurbān* or *qurb* that are often used to reference the sacrifice on Eid al-Adha literally mean to draw close to Allah ﷻ. This word is also used in Hebrew within the Jewish tradition, and symbolises a means of honouring the One God.

Ibn ʿUmar ﷺ narrates that the Prophet ﷺ stayed in Medina for ten years and offered the *uḍhi-yyah* every year (*Tirmidhī*), which demonstrates that although the Prophet ﷺ only performed a singular Hajj during his time in Medina on the 9th year after the Hijrah, he nevertheless offered a sacrifice every year that he resided in Medina. Similarly, the Prophet ﷺ would fast the Day of 'Arafah from the second year after Hijrah onwards, even prior to the establishment of Hajj as a religious obligation.

Connecting through sacrifice

For those who have been to 'Umrah or Hajj, we know that while we're in a state of *iḥrām*, there are certain prohibitions upon us, such as not being allowed to cut or diminish the length of our hair or nails. Similarly, when a person is not on Hajj, but intends to offer a sacrifice to commemorate the first 10 days of Dhul Hijjah, they're not allowed to shorten their hair or nails until after the sacrifice is complete.

The significance of this lies in the connection it builds between those who are performing Hajj and those who remain in their communities. Most of the time, those of us who are not on Hajj have a hard time connecting to the people who are undertaking the great pilgrimage and the profound rituals that they are performing. However, considering the prohibitions applied universally to those intending to offer a sacrifice, the one intending to offer the sacrifice becomes like the one who is in a state of *iḥrām* in this sense. Moreover, another benefit mentioned by al-Shawkānī ؈ in his book *Nayl al-Awṭār* is that just like the person in a state of *iḥrām* is completely ransomed from the punishment of Hell on the Day of Judgement, likewise, so too is the one offering a sacrifice ransomed by his sacrifice and protected from punishment on the Day of Judgement if it has been accepted by Allah ؈. Being in the state of the one who sacrifices thus frees your entire body from punishment and ransoms yourself with Allah ؈ as you offer that sacrifice.

It is imperative to note that it is the person offering the sacrifice, and not necessarily the one carrying it out or the one on behalf of whom it is being carried, who needs to be in this state. If I delegate someone else to carry out the sacrifice although I am the one offering the sacrifice, that person is not subject to the prohibitions of *iḥrām* – I am. Similarly, if I am offering a sacrifice on behalf of my family, I am bound by the prohibitions rather than them, although they will still benefit from the full reward of the sacrifice.

Communal feasts

The two occasions of Eid are a beautiful part of our religion that exemplify the brotherhood and sisterhood of Islam. When we celebrate Eid al-Fitr after the month of Ramadan comes to an end, we also distribute *zakāh al-fiṭr* – a charity that is due on every person that can afford it to pay for the feast of someone else. Financially able Muslims are required to give *zakāh al-fiṭr* so that the entire community is able to feast on the Day of Eid and enjoy their celebrations, especially if they are not otherwise able to feast throughout the year. Likewise, on Eid al-Adha, it is Sunnah for a person who is financially able to offer a sacrifice and distribute the meat to those who would typically not be able to feast on this special day.

In many countries around the world, Muslims are only able to eat meat on this day due to the distribution of the *uḍḥiyyah*, which demonstrates how beautiful it is that both of the occasions of Eid require us to include the wider community in our celebrations.

Accordingly, as is the case regarding Eid al-Fitr, if you can afford to feed your fellow Muslims, then you must do so. If you are able to offer a sacrifice so that others can enjoy the meat of that sacrifice and join the festivities of Eid, then you should do so, thereby allowing the entire community to truly enjoy Eid together. May Allah ﷻ allow us to see the benefits of *uḍḥiyyah* in this life and in the next, and join us with our beloved Prophet Muhammad ﷺ, Prophet Ibrāhīm ﷺ, and all the Prophets in the highest levels of Jannah al-Firdaws.

Indeed, my prayer, my rites of sacrifice, my living and my dying are for Allah, Lord of the worlds.

8

Three Years of Expiation

What if I told you that you could have three years of sins expiated in two days? What a blessing from Allah ﷻ indeed! The Prophet ﷺ informed us that when a person fasts on the Day of 'Arafah, Allah ﷻ will expiate the sins of the year before it and the year thereafter. The Prophet ﷺ further informed us that when a person fasts on the Day of 'Āshūrā', Allah ﷻ will expiate the sins of the year before it (*Muslim*).

What does that mean and how does this equate to three years? The Day of 'Arafah occurs in Dhul Hijjah, the last month of the Islamic year, and the Day of 'Āshūrā' occurs in Muḥarram, the first month of the Islamic calendar. Imagine, for example, that it's the year 1440 and you fast the Day of 'Arafah – Allah ﷻ will expiate the sins of the year before (1439) and the year after (1441). Once you move into Muḥarram, the first month of 1441, and you fast the Day of 'Āshūrā', Allah ﷻ will expiate the sins of the year before the Islamic New Year, 1440. As such, by fasting the Day of 'Arafah and the Day of 'Āshūrā', you would have had the sins of the years 1439, 1440, and 1441 expiated! It is a blessing from Allah ﷻ that these two months come side by side in the manner in which they do, and that Allah ﷻ expiates three years of sin as a result of this.

'Arafah and 'Ashura' in context

The Prophet ﷺ received revelation commanding him to fast the Days of 'Arafah and 'Āshūrā' very early on in the Medinan period. Allah ﷻ refers to this in the following verse of Sūrah al-Baqarah:

يَٰٓأَيُّهَا ٱلَّذِينَ ءَامَنُوا۟ كُتِبَ عَلَيْكُمُ ٱلصِّيَامُ كَمَا كُتِبَ عَلَى ٱلَّذِينَ مِن قَبْلِكُمْ لَعَلَّكُمْ تَتَّقُونَ ١٨٣ أَيَّامًا مَّعْدُودَٰتٍ

'O you who have believed, decreed upon you is fasting as it was decreed upon those before you that you may become righteous – [Fasting for] a limited number of days...' (al-Baqarah, 183-184).

The Qur'anic expression 'a few days' (or selected dates) refers to the days of 'Arafah and 'Āshūrā'. This verse marks the first legislation regarding fasting before Ramadan, although when these days were initially legislated people were given a choice whether to fast on these days or to give *fidyah* to feed a poor person instead. Unlike with Ramadan, people once had the option to choose whether they wanted to fast on 'Arafah and 'Āshūrā' – they could fast on those days, but were not obligated to do so, as they could alternatively give *fidyah* to feed a poor person for whichever fasts were not observed.

Subsequently, when the fast of Ramadan was prescribed, a choice was not given – fasting was made obligatory and *fidyah* was permitted only for those permanently unable to fast. When this ruling was enacted, fasting the days of 'Arafah and ʿĀshūrā' became entirely voluntary with *fidyah* inapplicable to either of the two days.

When you are unable to fast

Someone from the second generation of Muslims said to Ibn ʿAbbās ﷺ: 'What a strange thing that we have witnessed in you, O Companions of the Messenger of Allah ﷺ. We noticed that when you travel or you are sick during the days of Ramadan, you skip those days and break your fast, but we noticed that you fast these days of ʿArafah and ʿĀshūrā' even while you are travelling.'

Ibn ʿAbbās ﷺ responded, saying: 'Allah ﷺ says about the days of Ramadan, that whoever is travelling or unable to [fast] can simply make them up on other days and they would not be deprived of the reward, but there is no similar expiation or making-up for the days of ʿArafah and ʿĀshūrā'.' These two days only come once a year and have specific timings, so if a person can fast those days while they are travelling then they should.

What then, of those who cannot fast these days due to permanent illness or menstruation? Regarding this, the Prophet ﷺ said: 'Verily, Allah has recorded good and evil deeds, and He made them clear. Whoever intends to perform a good deed but does not do it [due to sickness, travel, or something out of their hands], Allah will record it as a complete good deed' (*Muslim*).

If a person would have fasted those days had they not been restrained due to circumstance, then Allah ﷻ in His infinite knowledge, mercy, and justice, will give them its full reward. They have the opportunity to do other good deeds that they have not been restricted from, and Allah ﷻ will still give them the reward of fasting these days without removing any of the blessings within them. Therefore, if you find yourself in this position, put your worries aside – do not be sad, thinking that you are being punished because you are unable to fast. Allah ﷻ has given you a gift and the reward is assured.

We ask Allah ﷻ to allow us to witness these days of fasting, and we ask Allah ﷻ to forgive us for whatever shortcomings we have, and we ask Allah ﷻ to grant us expiation not just for three years of sins, but for our entire lifetimes. *Āmīn.*

9

The Wonders of ʿArafah

The Day of ʿArafah is the most blessed day of the year; it is the day in which Allah ﷻ boasts to the Angels of His servants gathered together, all covered in dust and dirt, dishevelled and fatigued yet calling upon Him, invoking Him for His Mercy on the plains of ʿArafah and worldwide.

The Prophet ﷺ said: 'Hajj is ʿArafah' (*Tirmidhī*), which means that ʿArafah is the very heart of the Hajj. Contained in those blessed moments of ʿArafah is the essence of Hajj distilled into a single day. Just as the Prophet ﷺ declared that supplication is worship (*Tirmidhī*) and that 'regret is repentance' (*Ibn Mājah*) in order to indicate that the essence of true worship is sincere supplication and that the heart of true repentance is sincere regret, likewise, 'Arafah is the very summation of Hajj, and it has significance to all of us around the world.

It was narrated by 'Ā'ishah ﷺ that the Prophet ﷺ said: 'There is no day in which Allah sets free more souls from the fire of Hell than on the Day of 'Arafah' (*Muslim*). On that day, Allah ﷻ draws near to the Earth, and by way of exhibiting His pride, remarks to the Angels: 'What is it that these servants of Mine are asking Me for so that I may grant it to them? What is it that these servants of Mine are asking Me for?'

Imagine the sight of 'Arafah: four million people all making *du'ā*', all supplicating to Allah ﷻ in the same desert valley, all calling out to their Lord at the same time in all of their different languages, putting forth their most sincere requests in a thousand different tongues, being heard by the All-Hearing ﷻ, Who listens to each and every single one of them at that moment, answering their supplications. As they call out to Allah ﷻ with their hearts and with their souls, He does not deprive a single one of them. Imagine how blessed this occasion is: people all over the world yearn to be a part of it and call upon Allah ﷻ from wherever they are, begging Him for forgiveness, seeking His pleasure and bounty for everything in their lives, and in spite of the vast multitudes of worshippers, Allah ﷻ answers each and every single one of them.

Dear brothers and sisters, the benefits of Hajj and 'Arafah reach the entire Ummah. So pray for yourself, pray for your Ummah, pray for the people around the world, and let the benefits of this blessed day flow forth, God willing. Fasting this day is important; intensifying your prayers during this day is important; making *du'ā'* on this day is important; not committing any sins that might remove the blessings of this day is important.

Shaytan's humiliation

The Prophet ﷺ said to us: 'There is no day in the year in which the Shaytān is more humiliated and in more despair than he is on this day [the day of ʿArafah].' (*Mustadrak al-Ḥākim*)

Why is this? The reason is that he has been working for our entire lives to take us away from our Creator. Then, on this day, we call upon Allah ﷻ for a few hours, and Allah ﷻ forgives us for all of our sins. Allah ﷻ returns us to a noble ranking and good standing, causing all of Shaytān's efforts to delude us and lead us astray to be in vain. The Devil witnesses all of these people calling upon their Lord, being forgiven, leaving his demonic grasp and fleeing into the Mercy of Allah ﷻ, and he feels completely humiliated.

The Prophet ﷺ also mentioned that the only day that he was more humiliated than this was on the Day of Badr, when he saw Jibrīl ﷺ and his army descend. Shaytān thought that the battle of Badr would end Islam, but when he saw Jibrīl 🕮, he knew that he had been defeated. Likewise, each year the Day of 'Arafah arrives and he sees all of these Angels descending and the people being forgiven for their sins, and he knows that he has lost the battle with you as an individual.

Make this the day in which you completely stamp Shayṭān out of your life. May Allah 🕮 free you from any type of punishment and make you amongst those that He boasts about for earning His pleasure. May Allah 🕮 accept from us all this momentous occasion. *Āmīn*.

10

And in That Let Them Rejoice

We end the first ten days of Dhul Hijjah as we ended the last ten nights of Ramadan, in celebration of Allah's ﷻ mercy and the fact that we were given a chance to perform good deeds hoping to achieve His acceptance, and for the fact that we were given an opportunity to pray to Him and ask for forgiveness in the first place. Allah ﷻ states in Sūrah Yūnus:

قُل بِفَضلِ اللَّهِ وَبِرَحمَتِهِ فَبِذٰلِكَ فَليَفرَحوا
هُوَ خَيرٌ مِمّا يَجمَعون

"Say, 'In the bounty of Allah and in His mercy – in that let them rejoice; it is better than what they accumulate.'" (Yūnus, 58)

Rejoicing in the bounty and mercy of Allah ﷻ is greater than anything we can gather in this world. We have two occasions of Eid, two holidays or feasts in Islam: one Eid comes after the best ten nights; the other comes after the best ten days. One Eid comes after a month of fasting; the other, after ten days of good deeds. One Eid comes after Laylah al-Qadr, which is the best of the last ten nights and a night that is worth more than an entire lifetime. The other festival comes after the Day of ʿArafah, which is the best day of the year and a day during which we could be redeemed entirely in the sight of Allah ﷻ.

The position of these two days speaks to the fact that the two occasions of Eid come with acts of worship, and that there is something profound about the spirit of salvation in Islam: we are not commemorating someone else's good deeds or their acceptance by Allah ﷻ. Rather, we are commemorating Allah's ﷻ mercy and in the very fact that He allows us to perform good deeds, yearning for Him to accept our meagre endeavours because of that same mercy and grace from Him.

We take action during the 29 or 30 days of Ramadan and in these ten days of Dhul Hijjah, and then celebrate what Allah ﷻ allowed us to do. We celebrate His mercy and depend upon a good answer from Him. The Prophet ﷺ said: 'Call upon Allah with certainty that He will answer you'. We must be confident in Allah's ﷻ generous response whenever we do good deeds, not because of our supreme performance of them or any intrinsic virtue, but because of Allah's ﷻ boundless mercy in accepting them in spite of our faults.

Two joys

The Prophet ﷺ taught us to recite Sūrah al-Ḍuḥā and Sūrah al-Aʿlā during the Eid prayer, perhaps because within these chapters Allah ﷻ declares:

$$\text{وَلَلآخِرَةُ خَيْرٌ لَّكَ مِنَ الأُولَى}$$

'Indeed what is to come will be better for you than what is gone by.' (al-Ḍuḥā, 4).

وَالآخِرَةُ خَيْرٌ وَأَبْقَىٰ

'While the Hereafter is better and more enduring.'
(al-Aʿlā, 17).

The Hereafter is better than everything in this world and everything that it contains, and Eid – a celebration of worldly joys – is to celebrate what is greater than everything in this world: Allah's mercy, bounty, and forgiveness. The Prophet reminds us that the fasting person experiences two joys – the joy of breaking their fast, and the joy of meeting Allah with that fast completed (*Tirmidhī*). Similarly, for those who perform a sacrifice in Allah's name are two similar joys – the joy of eating the fruits of that sacrifice in this world, and the joy of meeting Allah with that sacrifice in the next.

May Allah accept our good deeds, our sacrifice, our remembrance, our fasting, and our charity in these ten days. May Allah accept our devotions on the Day of ʿArafah and allow us to be amongst those that are sanctified on the Day of Judgement and elevated to the highest level of Jannah al-Firdaws with the Prophets , whose examples we follow in drawing close to Him. May Allah allow us to dwell in that same level of Paradise and reside close to Him for all eternity. *Āmīn.*

Indeed what is to come will be better for you than what is gone by.

Notes

